The
SPIRITUAL
PSYCHIC

4 NECESSARY STEPS FOR
HEALERS & LIGHT WORKERS
TO PROTECT AGAINST
EVIL & DEMONS

NORA TRUSCELLO

This book was written for and dedicated to the explorer, who yearns to reach beyond physical limitations to meet personal guardians and spiritual counselors in God's realm of peace.

Table of Contents

ACKNOWLEDGMENTS

When I began writing my book, it was filled with thoughts, emotions, and experiences, all in the worst grammatical form one could image. Thanks to the patience, dedication, and brilliance of my daughter-law, Courtney Truscello, my writing now flows gracefully. While nursing her newborn son and being interrupted by her two-year-old son, more often than you can image, she managed to type, at times one-handed, all my thoughts into a cohesive book. With deepest appreciation, I acknowledge her beautiful heart and generous spirit.

Further acknowledgment must go to my husband, Anthony, who no matter my adventure or latest desire to explore, supports me every step of the way. Love is accepting a person for the way they are and accepting them for way they are not—my husband accepts me fully.

My final acknowledgment is to God, Christ, and the Holy Spirit. God for the enlightenment, Christ for the protection, and the Holy Spirit for His breadth of life.

INTRODUCTION

I'm *not* crazy . . .

This comforting realization settles over the victim of a spiritual attack when they realize what has happened to them was real and that they're not alone. Today, people are exploring not only our physical world, but the spiritual one as well. Just as ancient mariners had sextants to guide them through the seas, today's spiritual travelers need guidance as well. Without the proper knowledge and tools, those seeking spiritual and psychic enlightenment can leave themselves open to attack from forces wishing to do them harm. After an attack, victims are further alienated by the reluctance of those around them to believe that the attack even happened.

My goal in writing this book is to allow you to safely open the doors into the other realm in a way that will attract only loving, positive energy. The first part of my book focuses on what can go wrong if you travel unprotected into the spiritual realm. The second part of my book will teach you how to safely and successfully cross into the psychic world if you so choose.

The outcome of opening the wrong door can be horrific. In order to dissuade my readers from attempting any spiritual travel, even meditation, without the proper protection, I will share a few stories in which these wrong doors were unintentionally opened and my spiritual guidance was called upon to resolve the crises. These cases reflect incidents of physical illness, voodoo, incubus, and possession. Only the names and locations have been changed for privacy purposes. Sadly, not all of these cases ended happily, but they each provide an essential lesson.

If you choose to open the door into the other realm, it is crucial that you know how to protect yourself. The simple practice of meditation, when done incorrectly, can cause tremendous hardship for its practitioners. That being said, not everyone who meditates, visits a psychic, or learns to read tarot cards will be in danger, but these practices do increase the likelihood of falling prey to sinister forces when the practitioner is ill-prepared. Anyone can sit behind the wheel of a car, even a toddler. But not everyone will be ready or prepared to drive. Consider Part Two of my book your spiritual driver's education and defensive driving course wrapped into one.

In the Part Two protection section, the Lord's Prayer will be broken down and its protective powers explained. According to Edgar Cayce, known as the American Psychic and the Father of Holistic Medicine, reciting the Lord's Prayer has a direct effect on our chakra system. This is confirmed by Donna Eden, a best-selling author, teacher, and energy healer who can physically see the energy fields surrounding individuals. The Lord's Prayer protects and prepares the soul to travel safely. Using basic forms of energy work, such as strengthening our meridians, provides physical strength as well as spiritual protection. When these exercises are performed in conjunction with speaking Psalms, the level of protection reached will safeguard you not only in this world, but also the spirit world.

It is crucial to believe one thing above all else: Evil is REAL. As C. Norman Shealy, MD, PhD, founder and

CEO of the National Institute of Holistic Medicine, quoted after reviewing this book wrote, "There is no question that evil exists and can take over the mind and body. It is critically important to take care of yourself and to seek appropriate spiritual help when bizarre events and personality changes occur."

To deny the existence of evil will not protect you from it, but rather leave you more vulnerable. Denying the existence of cars will not protect you from getting hit by one if you walk into the street, just as denying the dangers of a thunderstorm will not protect you from getting struck by lightning. Evil preys on the ignorant, and we are unfortunately surrounded by it. We live in a world fraught with evil. In our own country, innocent unborn children are legally murdered every day under the justification of a woman's right to choose what happens to her body. A less commonly recognized form of evil is addiction. An addict is possessed by their addiction until it consumes them completely, stealing their free will, and the person they once were is replaced, often literally, but a demonic entity that torments any who try to help the addict.

For several years I had the pleasure of working with a small group called the Battered Boundaries Volunteers (BBV). Battered Boundaries was committed to helping people who had disturbing, intrusive, or otherwise unwanted, psychic experiences. The Battered Boundaries Volunteers were all members of the Edgar Cayce Foundation's Association of Research and Enlightenment (A.R.E.). For nearly twenty years, these volunteers were committed to helping those in spiritual crisis. When unusual calls came into the A.R.E that their call center was not trained to handle, the Battered Boundaries Volunteers were called to help. We helped the victims of bizarre psychic attacks reclaim their lives by helping them heal and transform these unrestrained, feral experiences into focused skills that they could control.

Battered Boundaries is based upon two concepts from the Edgar Cayce readings. The first concept is "All you meet is self" (Reed, "Battered Boundaries"). This concept teaches us to look within ourselves, rather than at outside circumstances, to find the source of our negative spiritual encounters. Cayce lays all responsibility for our lives squarely in our own laps. The second concept is that of affinity or "Like attracts like" (ibid.). Our thoughts are like magnets. When we send out negative energy and messages, we invite in more of the same. Once a door is opened to disturbing experiences, the negative energy created will attract more of the same, exponentially multiplying the uncontrollable psychic forces.

"Why me?" the victim often asked us despondently. The BBV's gentle response, "Let's find out." Using the two Cayce concepts, we helped the victim examine significant past experiences that caused them to feel afraid, threatened, or out of control. A key way we, volunteers, helped was through active listening. We reflected back to the victims, not only their words, but also the feelings and attitudes they expressed, helping them to become more aware of their own emotions. The process helped them to find the answers that were buried deep within by the ego in an attempt to protect itself from fully experiencing these terrible pains.

Through active listening and using our own intuitive psychic skills, we helped the victims begin to unravel their past and identify where a wound to their spirit or psyche had occurred. Once we could identify the nature of the wound and when it occurred, the volunteer would help the victim answer key questions: "What did they do to open this door into the unseen world?" and "How did this wound attract energies from the unseen world?" This is where the second concept of "Like attracts like" comes into play. If you are sending out anger, resentment, or, most commonly, fear into the open door, you will attract spirits and energies that match the frequency of these emotions.

I'm a devout Catholic, and I receive great comfort and strength from prayer. Prayer is a highly personal act, and there is no right or wrong way to go about it, but there are guidelines. God has somehow become an uncomfortable term in our culture, so many people pray to things other than God, for example mother earth. Unfortunately, it is easier for many to be politically correct than to stand up in their faith and embrace it.

Secular society has made it difficult to appreciate our religious upbringing and spiritual traditions. Edgar Cayce said that in order to excel in your spiritual growth it is best to practice the religion you were born into. He reasoned that we pick that religion before coming into this earthly realm because we have something we need to gain from it.

The final part of my book tells my own story and how my life experiences led me to become a Battered Boundaries Volunteer. When I was in my early twenties, there were such extremely negative psychic energies acting on me that I physically felt like I was dying. The physical pain I experienced was so deep that I was convinced I was suffering from some unknown illness. However, the lessons I gained from my difficult experiences allow me today to do healings, spiritual clearings, and psychic readings, all through the power of prayer.

Next . . .

Our first story is about Liz, a woman from South Carolina who had a voodoo curse cast upon her that wrecked havoc on her life for over twenty years . . .

PART ONE

HARD LESSONS

1 - Why Curses Work

The Edgar Cayce Foundation's Association of Research and Enlightenment (ARE) received a call from a mother in South Carolina, hoping to get help for her daughter, Liz. Due to the severity of Liz's situation, her call was allocated to the ARE's most experienced unit, the Battered Boundaries Volunteers (BBV), of which I was a part.

Liz, who was 42, had been experiencing one strange accident after another for the past twenty plus years. No sooner would Liz heal from one injury, then she would suffer a new one. Once she fell down the stairs and broke her ankle. A week after healing, she broke several ribs in a car accident. These bizarre, back-to-back accidents prevented Liz from holding down a job or getting involved in a serious relationship. More often than not, Liz was bedridden from the accidents and illnesses that plagued her.

Liz's physician could not find a medical explanation as to why or how one person could experience such a continuous slew of illness and injury. He believed that Liz must be under the attack of some type of negative energy. He suggested, off the record, that Liz call the A.R.E. for guidance.

As Liz, herself, had no energy to speak, for over an hour, her mother, Lucy, painted for me the disturbing picture that was her daughter's life. I learned that Liz had served in the military and been honorably discharged twenty years previously. Upon being discharged, Liz met a handsome young man named Aaron who courted her. Liz quickly fell in love, only to discover that Aaron was married and had children. Despite Aaron's persistence, Liz broke off the relationship. Feeling jilted and heartbroken, Aaron paid to have a voodoo curse cast upon Liz, giving him possession over her and disabling Liz from ever being with anyone else or having a life without him. Aaron quickly went on with his life and never gave the curse much thought again. He eventually forgot about it completely.

Though I learned a lot about Liz from her mother, I was unable to ask her the essential questions that would provide me the needed insight as to why Liz experienced such continuous suffering. I promised Lucy that the A.R.E. prayer group that I was (and am) a member of, called In Search of God, would hold Liz in our prayers, asking God to heal her and bring back her strength. Without access to Liz, I had to leave her recovery in God's hands.

When I called a week later for a follow-up, I learned that Liz was up and about, walking her dog, sewing with her sister, and overall feeling immensely better than she had felt in years. With her strength restored, I was finally able to speak directly with Liz. Almost immediately, she asked the often heard but always heartrending question, "Why me?" Together, we did some deep soul-searching, and within an hour we had our answer.

Liz had made an unconscious decision that she was unworthy of happiness because of her experiences during the war. Though physically unharmed, Liz was left mentally wounded and didn't feel that she had a right to be happy when other members of her troop were left with permanent physical injuries. Liz was sending out a negative, unspoken message to the universe—"I don't deserve to be happy."

When the voodoo curse was cast, opening the door to the other side, Liz's negative thoughts caused her to be bombarded by negative energies. Liz couldn't have prevented the curse from being cast, but, if she had been sending out a positive message of Godly love and gratitude, nothing evil or negative would have been attracted through the open door.

Liz was thrilled and relieved to finally have an understanding of why she experienced repeated difficulties. She decided to get professional help to support her in moving past her guilt that came from leaving the military unharmed. My prayer group continued to pray for her and her family to ensure that the voodoo curse was completely dissipated and that the door that had been opened was sealed.

Lucy was elated with how the BBV had turned her daughter's life around. She proceeded to ask if I would help her other daughter who was living across the country and struggling with her housekeeper, who was involved in the evil practices of Santeria. Lucy pleaded that I force this housekeeper out with the same power I had used to free Liz. I tried in vain to explain to Lucy that it was the power of prayer that had freed Liz from her curse, along with Liz's desire and willingness to change her life. Lucy refused to understand the power of free will and that I had no right to impose her will on anyone else. Lucy failed to see the irony of her request—that Aaron had imposed his will upon Liz for twenty years with his curse and now Lucy wanted me to do something similar to her other daughter's housekeeper. Upon closing this case, I felt comfortable in knowing that at least Liz understood free will and was taking the necessary steps to take back control of her life.

Lessons To Learn

Curses are real; they work—even a simple curse muttered under one's breath in passing. The level of intention is what is important. Aaron was extremely angry and greatly wanted his curse to work. The fact that he paid for it also represents a strong level of intention. Equally important is the fact that even though Aaron lost interest in Liz after a few months, his curse continued to work its harmful magic.

If we intentionally send out hatred, it does harm to its intended. When you wish harm upon the driver who cuts you off in traffic, it affects them. If the driver is suffering from an unhealed spiritual wound, then wishing them harm opens a door that will attract with magnitude whatever hurt they are sending out into the universe back to them.

It is not only our words that can cause harm, but also our thoughts. The Apostle Paul in 2 Corinthians 10:4–5 spoke of taking every thought captive, "We are destroying speculations and every lofty thing raised up against the knowledge of God, and we are taking every thought captive to the obedience of Christ." Our thoughts are extremely powerful. We must guard ourselves against our thoughts lazily flowing through our heads. If we practice bringing mindfulness to our actions, we can stop the havoc-causing chatter that runs unrestrained through our heads. In 1 Thessalonians 5:17, the Apostle Paul said, "Pray without ceasing" (KJV). Being in a constant state of prayer allows us to control our thoughts and guard ourselves from unintentionally harming others with the careless chatter our minds create.

It is important to understand that even if a curse is thrown your way, as long as you protect yourself, you won't fall harm to the malevolence that the curse intended. Our thoughts and emotions work like a beacon, sending out energy into the universe and attracting more of the same. Liz was not protected because she was sending out feelings of being unworthy and unhappy. Her emotional wound attracted more of the same unhappiness when Aaron opened a door with his curse. If Liz had, instead, been full of Godly love, she would have been protected and Aaron's curse would have merely been a waste of money.

NEXT . . .

In my next case, no voodoo was needed to open a door. Sam's curiosity to explore the psychic and spiritual realms was all that was needed to open her up to partial possession.

2 - Bearing False Gifts

S am and Ed, who were both on their second marriage, were living in an 1880s homestead in rural Pennsylvania. At the time of the intervention, they had two children together, an 8-year-old son and a 10-year-old daughter. Ed called the ARE, desperately seeking help for his wife who had been spontaneously dropping to the floor, curling into a ball, grinding her teeth, and foaming at the mouth.

Through Ed, we learned that ever since Sam had attended a psychic fair a few months previously and learned how to release spirits, their marriage and home life had been rapidly deteriorating. Ed said their home recently became filled with clutter up to his waist, and Sam's obsession with releasing spirits was causing her to neglect her family. I had to learn as much as I could about this case through Ed because Sam initially believed that speaking with me would disrupt her work. I understood her resistance because, when done properly, spirit releasement is God's work.

Spirit releasement is assisting a ghost to make its way into the light if it failed to do so upon death. After dying, many spirits will linger for as long as three days before they come to peace with the realization that they have died. By the third day after their passing, a spirit will be compelled to move toward God's light where it will find mercy and rest according to its deeds on Earth.

However, countless souls fail to move into the light for a myriad of reasons. We refer to these lost souls as ghosts. Two of the most common reasons for not crossing over are the fear of being judged and the denial that one is dead. Though not forgotten by God, these ghosts continue to roam the realm of the living by their own free will. God, in His unconditional love, will not impose His will on these lost souls by forcing them into the light. Their will to stay on this earth is honored by God, even though by choosing to stay, a spirit only prolongs its own suffering.

Over the years, my spiritual psychic partner, Christine Gurganus, and I have released thousands of ghosts. I have worked with groups of extremely loving people who, purely out of the goodness of their hearts, give vast amounts of their time and energy to help ghosts move on. Releasing spirits is not difficult. It just requires a great amount of focus and prayer in order to help the ghost see the mercy that is God's light. A group must pray constantly until the home, community, or geographical region is cleared. Sadly, this work will never end because so many lack faith in a superior being. Upon death, these souls believe they have no other choice than to aimlessly wander our world.

Sam finally agreed to speak with me under the condition that I promise not to interfere with her daily practice of remotely releasing spirits. Remote releasing is to allow your own spirit to leave your body and travel to the desired location in order to personally assist a soul or souls to cross into the light. As I developed my own spirituality, I stopped using this dangerous technique as it leaves the traveler susceptible to partial possession. I now rely totally on the power of prayer to do spirit releasement. I promised Sam that I wouldn't interfere, not realizing it would prevent her from accepting help in the future.

During our first conversation, we looked into why Sam seemed to be suffering from seizures when she had no unusual medical conditions. I asked her if there were any times during her childhood in which she felt like she was out of control. Sam proudly stated that she was never out of control, that she had always been a responsible and level-headed child. Sam was born right in the middle of a family of eleven children. She had never received gifts on her birthday or holidays. It didn't seem to upset Sam who reasoned that it was because her parents knew she understood their difficult financial situation, and they could save money by not giving her presents.

I offered a possible theory as to Sam's behavior based on my education and life experiences. I do not claim to have any formal training in psychology, and I made that clear to Sam. I suggested that her inner child could possibly be acting out after years of feeling neglected. Sam didn't believe that was the cause. She said she never felt neglected and refused to discuss that matter further.

We looked again into her past and Sam told me that her parents' busy lives often made it difficult for them to show her much attention. She did, however, have one uncle who showed her a great deal of attention. This uncle took Sam to different places, showed her love, and treated her specially. Then one day, her uncle exposed himself sexually to her. Sam told her father, and, in return, her father never talked to her again. Sam said she had never shared this with her therapist. It shocked me that she had never shared this deep wound with the one person in the world who was most likely and capable of helping her.

When Sam's soul traveled to assist lost souls, she left her body unprotected and open to invasion. The years of neglect, along with Sam's own father's failure to protect her, caused her internal beacon to send out signals of rejection and being unworthy of love. Those vibrations were attracted back to her tenfold.

Sam shared with me that most nights she felt compelled to lay naked in the moonlight on top of a large rock that was alongside a stream. For hours every night, a spirit talked to her, sharing secrets about energy that it claimed were vital to mankind. Sam was instructed to transcribe the messages in secret, until an unknown time in the future when she'd be instructed to present them to the world. Sam was convinced that she was specially chosen to be entrusted with this great knowledge.

Intuitively, I understood that Sam was channeling a sinister spirit that had disguised itself as good. I knew that in order for Sam to be able to protect herself, she first needed to become mentally stronger. I encouraged Sam to share everything she had disclosed to me with her counselor. Sam willingly agreed. We planned to talk again in one week.

During that time, I risked traveling in spirit to Sam and Ed's home in order to have a better understanding of the force that Sam was up against. I was intuitively warned not to travel without first having an extended period of prayer for grace. As my spirit approached their home, protective forces blocked me from moving too close. The energy surrounding their home was so intense that I immediately knew there was evil present.

We all have sensors on our bodies that alert us when evil is present. Their location is unique to each person. Once we identify where our sensors are, they never fail us. I learned this technique from Carol Ann Liaros, a master teacher of psychic abilities and the lead psychic at the A.R.E. for many years.

Upon returning to my own body, I prayed for the protection of everyone I knew and loved. I felt like I couldn't stop praying. On the rare occasion when one comes face to face with evil, it feels as though you can't ever pray enough to clear out all the negativity. But that is, of course, not true.

Before the week was up, Sam called to inform me that she had decided not to speak with her counselor. The spirit that Sam was communicating with had warned her that the counselor and I were dangerous and that we were trying to stop Sam from doing her work. I innately knew this spirit was evil but could see it would be pointless to tell Sam.

Instead, I asked her to tell me about all the work she did for the spirit. Sam told me that when she left her body, she lowered her soul into hell to release the souls that were trapped there by mistake. She helped release them into our earthly realm, so that they could complete their journeys. When I asked Sam if she believed God would make such a mistake, she promptly hung up on me.

Ed then called, begging me not to give up on his wife. He worried that his family would be ripped apart by the force he believed to be controlling his wife's will. From my experience, however, nothing Sam was doing appeared to be against her own will.

I have no right to go against anyone's free will, but, since there were young children in danger, I knew I had to seek help from an expert. I contacted a world-renowned demonologist through her museum's Facebook page and explained to her the situation. She called me within minutes, extremely concerned for the children, as was I. From there, I left the family in her hands.

A week later Sam called me, furious that I had gone against my promise not to try to stop her from doing her work. She said she would no longer talk to the demonologist or to me. There was nothing further either of us could do to try to help Sam.

Since no one can force their will on another and since Sam was unwilling to receive help, I sadly had to let go of this case. Afterward, I heard once from Ed that Sam was still journaling the spirit's messages, releasing spirits from hell, and completely neglecting her family. Ed said he was planning on taking the children away to raise them somewhere safe.

LESSONS TO LEARN

During her childhood, Sam endured deep emotional wounds from the neglect and rejection she experienced from her parents. This wound was further exacerbated when her father stopped speaking to her after Sam sought his protection from her uncle. Sam didn't consciously realize how affected she was from these childhood experiences. But her psyche did, and it cried out for attention and respect. Sam was not sending out a signal of Godly love, but rather the signal of an emotionally needy and wounded child.

When Sam first opened a door through remotely releasing spirits, she was completely vulnerable to the attack of a greedy, malevolent spirit wishing to use her for its own evil purpose. This sinister spirit gave Sam the sense of love and importance she had been craving and, in return, easily manipulated her to do its nefarious work. The spirit protected her newfound happiness by convincing Sam to chase away anyone trying to stop her from doing her work.

This is not a clear-cut case of possession. In order to be fully possessed, one must completely surrender one's free will. Once a soul is fully possessed, there is no hope of exorcising the demon because the person now wills for the possession. I wish I could say that Sam had accepted help and lived happily ever with her husband and children, but I am sure that is not the case. Spiritual travel, meditation, reiki, and other New Age modalities are all dangerous if you don't have the proper training to send out the appropriate Godly signals.

NEXT . . .

The next story is Susan's. This woman faced a very different kind of malicious entity. This spirit played on Susan's feelings of guilt that came from enduring a childhood wrought with violent sexual abuse. Susan found herself being physically raped and beaten by the spirit.

3 - WHAT DID I DO TO DESERVE THIS?

S usan wants her story to impress upon others how having unhealed wounds to the psyche can send out the wrong message to the spiritual world. Susan wrote a book about her horrific experience of being tortured and raped by a spirit.

Susan was not sent to me through the A.R.E. but by a fellow psychic who told me about her case. This psychic asked me to help because she knew about my work with extraordinary and unusual psychic phenomena. I set up an appointment to speak with Susan the very next day.

As always, I started the conversation by asking Susan why she believed this might be happening to her. Her response brought me to my knees, "Because it happened before." Susan's was, hands down, the worst case of child abuse and rape that I had ever encountered. Her parents were truly sadistic. Susan's father taught her brother to beat and rape her and her sister, Sharon, on a daily basis. The father also participated in the daily beatings and rapes. The sisters were kept like prisoners. Shockingly, their mother was completely complacent to this criminally sick behavior.

Though Susan could not even help her own self, she tried, in vain, to protect her sister, Sharon, from the abuse. Eventually Susan ran away from home and got married in order to escape the abuse. Though Sharon too eventually escaped from the physical abuse, she couldn't live with the mental and emotional scars. Sharon committed suicide when she was 32. I asked Susan if she had any memories of a happier time, but even her earliest memories were of abuse and rape.

The two hours we spent on the phone flew by as Susan poured out her heart to me. She described a childhood riddled with abuse and depression. In her home there had been a complete disregard for her and Sharon's welfare. As we spoke, I prayed silently that my intuition lead me to address what needed healing. I felt compelled to ask Susan if she had ever asked herself, "What did I do to deserve this?" In that moment, the woman I was talking to seemed to melt away into a sad, scared little girl who answered, "Yes, a million times."

I found it so profoundly sad that Susan's inner child believed she had done something to deserve abuse. I told Susan her repetitive thinking that she had done something to deserve abuse had sent out a signal to the universe, attracting more abuse. Susan was quick to see that the abuse was not her fault, but rather her father's. Her father was an extremely disturbed man who abused all of his children, including his son, for his own sick pleasure. He ruined all of his children's lives—his son, who has to live with the hideous acts he was forced to do as a child and young man; Susan's sister, Sharon, who took her own life; and Susan, who subconsciously believed that she deserved abuse and, therefore, continued to attract it into her life even as an adult.

When we spoke, Susan was happily married to her second husband. Her husband, Charlie, believed that she was under spiritual attack but found it difficult to understand how or why a spirit would do such a thing. He was also confused about how a spirit could be doing this when he was asleep in the same bed as his wife.

I explained that these demons are able to cast a heavy, paralyzing sleep over people. If you have ever experienced a dream in which you knew you were dreaming but were unable to move or wake yourself up, you may have been experiencing this type of demonic attack. There was one night when Charlie awoke and was horrified to see his wife being thrown around their bedroom though he could see no one else in the room. Another time, Charlie took his bleeding wife to the emergency room after a particularly violent rape, only to find himself under suspicion of having committed the attack.

The type of demonic spirit that attacked Susan is called an incubus. An incubus is a spirit that takes the form of a male in order to rape a woman. The female form of this spirit is called a succubus. According to the *Zohar*, one of the ancient books of the Kabbalah, demons disguise themselves as human to have sex with an unsuspecting person. The children of such a union retain their demonic nature and hold a high position within the kingdom of spirits. To conceive one of these children is often the reason for the sexual attack.

I understood how Susan's spiritual beacon had attracted such a demonic entity, but now we needed to figure out what had caused a door to be opened that let in this demon. According to Susan, her problems began when her family moved into their current apartment. No sooner were they settled into their new home did they start noticing objects moving around by themselves and felt an eerie presence. Trapped by their lease and tight finances, the family stayed in the apartment. Unbeknownst to them, a previous tenant of their apartment had opened a portal into the psychic realm. Therefore, the personal beacon of anyone who entered the apartment was calling out to the other side. Susan's beacon of "I deserve abuse" was being responded to.

Luckily for Susan and her family, this was one of my easier cases to solve. Despite all her years of being abused, Susan had an extremely forgiving heart. She had even forgiven her mother for all her years of passivity. Susan began to regain control of her life through prayer. Together, we prayed to Jesus, and I had her repeat over and over, "I am a child of God, deserving of His love, and I will accept nothing less." Susan accepted into her heart the truth that none of the abuse was her fault and that she was merely the victim of a sick man's deranged form of pleasure.

Susan reset her beacon to one of deserving happiness and Godly love. Immediately the demon challenged Susan's newfound strength by appearing in front of her, breathing in her face. For the first time, it was unable to touch her, and Susan knew she was finally free. By our next conversation a week later, Susan said she had the demon backed up against a wall and aware that it had lost all the power it had once held over her.

Susan has since written three books and is a flourishing author. Susan says she will always remember the difference God made in her life on that day she regained control.

LESSON TO LEARN

From years of repetition, Susan's beacon was sending out an extremely strong signal of "I deserve abuse." The amazing grace is that we can start to change our internal beacon the second we acknowledge the unconscious conversation that we have allowed to control our lives.

Susan's willingness to forgive her abusers for over a decade of horrendous abuse is truly inspirational. I believe it was why she was so quickly able to reclaim control over her life. If she had failed to forgive, her beacon would have changed from "I deserve abuse" to "I am angry" and angry forces would have been attracted into her life.

Those who have hurt us often don't care whether we forgive them or not. Forgiveness is truly a gift to ourselves. When we forgive, we let go of anger that has built up inside of us, the anger that was making us sick and attracting negativity into our lives.

Though I advocate forgiveness, I don't advocate forgetting. When we allow ourselves, we learn and grow from our difficult experiences, and, like Susan through her books, we can even make a positive difference in the lives of others.

NEXT . . .

At times, it is not one's inner beacon that calls forth a spirit, but the intentional channeling of a spirit. This created a nightmare scenario for Romulus who invited a spirit to attack him, rather than attacking the child he was trying to protect.

4 - GOOD INTENT ISN'T GOOD DEFENSE

This story is the perfect lead to the second part of the book, as it is the strongest example of the protective power of prayer that I have ever experienced. Only the names and locations have been changed. I picked the mystical name Romulus because it perfectly depicts the male protagonist in our story. Romulus is rugged, yet quiet and gentle. He's a highly intelligent, whiskey-drinking, tobacco-chewing, spiritual warrior with a pet wolf. For his wife, I chose the name Alena because it means light.

Romulus and Alena were living the American dream. They had three children, ran their own business, and enjoyed driving their Harleys together. No outsider would suspect that they communicated with the dead on a daily basis. Almost every night, these two travelled, sometimes as much as six hours round-trip, in order to help those in spiritual crisis. What is even more impressive is that they never asked for a dime. Helping those in need was all the payment they desired.

I had the pleasure of working with Romulus and Alena on several different cases. Our partnership helped me feel more comfortable in my own abilities. Romulus and Alena worked as a team to help spirits pass on. Romulus channeled the energy of the spirits, allowing them to speak through him. Alena spoke to the spirits with the sternness of a schoolteacher combined with the love of a mother, giving them the guidance and counsel they needed to move into the light. Occasionally a spirit resisted so strongly that Romulus and Alena called upon the help of their spirit guide, Amar. Their guide appeared not as an angel, but a fierce warrior dressed for battle. He had been helping Romulus and Alena, keeping them safe from the other side, for as long as they could remember.

Years of channeling spirits through his own body had taken a physical toll on Romulus. Alena begged him for years not to use this method but eventually surrendered to his stubbornness. Though they could both hear and communicate with the spirits without the use of channeling, Romulus continued to do this because he believed it gave him control over the spirits and kept them from harming anyone in the home. Channeling a spirit allows the spirit to feed off of the channel's energy by entering the channeler's body to communicate more effectively. It is extremely dangerous.

One day, Joseph, the head of our paranormal group, asked me to assist in a house clearing, in New York. My presence was often requested whenever a family would need extensive spiritual counseling in order to understand what was happening to them. As I, myself, am a mother of three boys, I immediately agreed to help when I learned that two young brothers were the center of this case. As soon as I stepped foot in the affected home, I was engulfed by a sense of dread. A palpable heaviness filled the quaint little house to the brim.

I immediately began to pray. I prayed silently as I listened to the brothers' account of how they had played with a Ouija board inside of a cemetery. I was still praying when the last member of our paranormal team, Christine Gurganus, arrived. Christine Gurganus, which is her real name, is one of the most accurate psychics I've ever met.

She is currently my good friend and partner in almost all of my spiritual clearings. Though I knew of the work she did with spirit releasement, I had never experienced Christine's method until that night.

Christine lit a smudge stick and began walking around the first floor, murmuring softly under her breath. Curious, I asked her what she was doing. She answered nonchalantly, "Praying, of course." I was pleasantly surprised by her answer. I had never met anyone else, either in the A.R.E. or the various other paranormal groups I had worked with, who talked openly about prayer. Many use prayer but keep it to themselves, as did I until I met Christine. I was in awe of this woman who openly prayed as she walked around with her smudge stick.

The smudge stick was releasing a layer of smoke so thick that we couldn't see each other from a mere two feet away. This was a clear indication of the massive amount of negative energy that was present and feeding off of the family's fear. I sensed this would be a difficult clearing and knew we would need all the help we could get. I took comfort in knowing there were two of us praying, for as Jesus says in the Bible, "For where two or three have gathered together in My name, I am there in their midst" (Matthew 18:20, New American Standard Bible).

As the group moved through the house, the dark energy kept evading us. Whenever we entered a room, the spirits would leave to avoid detection. They sensed we were trying to force them out, so they avoided us for fear of the judgment that awaited them upon entering the light. All the members of the group sensed that these were no ordinary spirits in need of some simple guidance, but rather a dark entity that the boys unintentionally attracted through playing with the Ouija board.

After trying unsuccessfully for hours to communicate, Romulus saw one of the dark entities trying to harm one of the brothers. He challenged the spirit to enter his own body in an attempt to keep the boy safe. There was an immediate and frightening change in Romulus. He seemed to have grown a foot in width and height, and his face distorted until we could no longer recognize him as our gentle friend. He stretched up like a creature intent on causing harm as Joseph and Mark, two other men in our group, tried in vain to hold him down. I went to him and placed my hands on his shoulders. I cried out, over and over, "Saint Michael, Saint Michael, help us!" Christine put her hands on Romulus and joined me in calling on Saint Michael while Alena called on Amar. Calling on St. Michael allowed us to lower Romulus into a chair without exerting any physical force. By the time he was seated, the entity that was inside Romulus had left his body.

The entire episode lasted less than a minute, but in that moment time stood still. Never once did I allow myself to be overcome with fear, for I have been trained not to fear the darkness. However, once it was all over, I was left shaking in panic. I believe that had Saint Michael not been called upon, we may have all been seriously injured. I imagined having to go home to my husband and tell him that my friend had hurt me or another in our group. Romulus's methods had endangered everyone in our group, and, from that point on, I decided to never participate in another clearing with Romulus and Alena.

A week later, my phone rang. It was the mother of the two boys, crying and begging me to help them. I apologized, explaining that I no longer worked with the group, but as she insisted, the voice within me pleaded, "Don't abandon them yet."

When I agreed to return, I was immediately filled with dread and anger. In my head, I yelled at God, "What have you gotten me into? Why did you encourage me say yes?" A startling thought occurred to me—what if it wasn't God's voice telling me to go, but that of the malevolent spirit, attempting to lure me into a trap? Realizing fear was guiding my thoughts, I decided to meditate for guidance.

During my meditation, Saint Michael spoke directly to me. He told me to ask Joseph and Mark to return with me to the affected house. I was instructed to say the Lord's Prayer over Joseph, Mark, and myself, one at a time. Then we were to enter the house but not communicate with the spirits in any way. Mark, who had the gift of sight, could, however, tell us what the spirits were doing. While praying with the mother and sons, we were to stand in a circle and order the spirits into our circle where they would be handled by God. Joseph would lead us in prayer, focusing solely on getting the spirits to come into the circle. Saint Michael instructed me that if Joseph or Mark were to deviate from his plan in any way, "Go immediately, leave them to the harsh lesson they must learn."

Joseph and Mark met me at the house. As instructed, I blessed each one of us. Before entering the home, I told Joseph in no uncertain terms that if Saint Michael's instructions were not followed to a T, I would walk out, leaving him and Mark to deal with the consequences. As soon as we entered the house, the first spirit appeared at the top of the stairs. Out of habit, Mark began to speak for the spirit, so I reminded him not to communicate, only to say what he sees. We began to pray, asking repeatedly that these spirits sense God's mercy and love.

After five minutes, the first spirit moved into the circle where it immediately ascended into the light. We were overcome with relief to know that these entities were not as evil or powerful as we had feared. We knew this because evil would not move on so quickly. The second spirit moved on almost as easily. The third spirit was a bit more challenging, but once we got it to enter the circle, Mark saw a mighty angel appear, lift up the spirit, and carry it away.

Within twenty minutes of our arrival, we had the house cleared of spirits and filled with Godly light. What I got out of this experience was how incredible and protective the power of prayer truly is. Faith and prayer are all we need to do God's work in helping spirits to pass on.

LESSONS TO LEARN

NEVER channel a spirit through your body. Romulus became a danger to himself and everyone in our paranormal group when he decided to allow a spirit to enter him. We are not capable of controlling a spirit, just as we cannot control another's will. Prayer and calling on Saint Michael had undoubtedly been our saving grace.

I cannot emphasize enough how imperative it is to say prayers of protection before beginning any kind of spiritual work. When working with dark and angry forces, continuous prayer is necessary throughout the entire process. Lastly, show no fear in the presence of evil. Fear is energy that angry forces are attracted to because they feed off of it. The exorcist, Father Gary Thomas, often begins lectures by saying, "Satan has been defeated." Holding this truth in one's heart removes all fear.

Lastly, do not EVER play with a Ouija board. Ouija boards open a door to the other side, and you never know what may come through.

PART ONE CLOSING THOUGHTS

One body, one soul. God created one body for each of us and one soul to occupy that body. Sharing that space is dangerous. A spirit can become attached and refuse to leave. It can eventually push its own desires and agenda on its host without the host's knowledge.

Someone close to me was involved in a serious car accident when she was five. I will call her Teresa after her favorite saint. A disincarnate spirit saw Teresa lying on the sidewalk after the crash. The spirit felt sorry for Teresa and went to her side, hoping to provide comfort and protection to the little girl. Teresa suffered a concussion and two broken legs. Those injuries would heal in time, but the emotional scar from losing her brother would take much longer.

Growing up, Teresa had an incredible gift for music. After hearing a song only once, she could play it on the piano from memory. However, Teresa struggled socializing with others. Around fifty years after the accident, she asked Christine and me to do a clearing on her home. During the clearing, we discovered the spirit that had been attached to Teresa since childhood. Teresa thanked it for wanting to help her but explained that it was time to move into the light. With prayer and singing, the spirit left Teresa. Since that day, she has had no problem communicating with others and has a fulfilling social life.

Teresa never invited the spirit to attach to her, but she lost control over her life all the same. An attachment is different from possession, but, once a spirit attaches to a person, it always causes interference in the host's life. As long as the spirit is attached, a remnant, if not the entire spirit, always remains until released by prayer.

NEXT . . .

In the next part of my book, I will teach you how to protect yourself from danger as you embark on the journey of discovering your highest self. I will teach you the four ways in which you can move safely in and out of these psychic realms.

Part Two

THE FOUR STEPS

5 - IDEALS AND HUMILITY

Before traveling into the psychic realms, there are four steps you must take to put yourself into a protected and sacred place.

First, you must pick an ideal you wish to strive towards.
Second, let go of personal desires to humble your ego.
Third, energetically prepare your physical body.
Fourth, call on Christ to bring you guidance and wisdom on your journey.

THE FIRST STEP: PICK AN IDEAL.

An ideal is not a goal. It is a motivational standard by which to evaluate our goals and our reasons for pursuing those goals. The goal is what; the ideal is why! A spiritual ideal is not so much a goal toward which we move as it is the spirit in which we grow. It is a living and dynamic standard by which we quicken and measure our daily motivation. (Puryear, H. B., Meditation and the Mind of Man, 112)

An ideal is a person or thing regarded as perfect. In the teachings of Edgar Cayce, he speaks of finding your spiritual ideal. You must hold this ideal in your heart when moving within the realms of meditation or spiritual exploration. It is important that your ideal is not one that can be attained, but always strived towards. In doing so, you strengthen your relationship with God.

For years, my personal ideal has been the Blessed Mother. Humble and graceful, she was the perfect servant of mankind. This is an ideal that can never be met, but she serves as a sort of spiritual lighthouse. She is a beacon of light and love that gets me through life's roughest storms.

Be careful to choose an ideal that is pure of heart. If your ideal is too rooted in earthly desires, it will wreak havoc on your soul and personal life. Whether your ideal be Christ, Ghandi, Mother Theresa, or another, your pursuit of this ideal will purify your soul, creating beauty and love in your life as you travel safely beyond this earthly realm.

THE SECOND STEP: LET GO OF PERSONAL DESIRES. HUMBLE YOUR EGO.

Ego is not good or evil, it is merely part of what makes us human. Ego is essential to healthy self-preservation. It is also what drives us to achieve great things.

Many great New Age teachers are misguided in their understanding of ego. They teach that ego is the root of evil. However, ego was created by God, and nothing of God can be evil. It is only when ego becomes out of control, focusing too intently on earthly and personal desires, that it can become problematic. We can train our egos to look past our own desires in order to be of service to others and God. With time and training, the practice of putting others before ourselves becomes effortless. When our ego is grounded and focused on serving others, we become strong in our faith and less likely to be swayed by frivolities or evil.

You may be wondering, "How do I go about training my ego?" A simple way to do this is to control how you react in trying situations. When a person or situation moves you to anger, take a moment to breathe and think about how God would want you to handle yourself.

Many Christians believe this means that they are always supposed to turn the other cheek. Though this is often a good course of action, it is not always the right thing to do. When the cause is a good one, you are allowed to be angry, just as Jesus was angered by the wrongdoings going on in the temple:

And Jesus entered the temple and drove out all those who were buying and selling in the temple, and overturned the tables of the money changers and the seats of those who were selling doves. And He said to them, "It is written, 'MY HOUSE SHALL BE CALLED A HOUSE OF PRAYER'; but you are making it a ROBBERS' DEN." (Matthew 21:12)

After practicing this simple ego training for a month, you will find much more joy in your life. Compassion and understanding will flow through you, and your will will be to do God's will.

THE THIRD STEP: PREPARE THE BODY.

Just as we prepare our minds and souls, we must also prepare our bodies. The body is composed of several energy systems that work together to protect us and keep us strong. Taking care of our energy systems is just as important as taking care of our physical bodies. As this is an extremely important concept, I have dedicated all of chapter six to it.

THE FOURTH STEP: CALL ON CHRIST.

Prayer is the strongest protection we can offer ourselves. Edgar Cayce's teachings say that calling on Jesus Christ will give you the utmost protection and allow you to communicate directly with God. Father Paul O'Sullivan, O.P., speaks of the power in just speaking the name of Jesus against evil:

The great, great evil, the great danger that threatens each of us every day and every night of our lives, is the devil. St. Peter and St. Paul warn us in the strongest language to beware of the devil, for he is using all his tremendous power, his mighty intelligence to ruin us, to harm, to hurt us in every way. There is no danger, no enemy in the world we have to fear as we should fear the devil. He cannot attack God, so he turns all his implacable hatred and malice against us. We are destined to take the thrones he and the other Bad Angels have lost. This lashes him into wild fury against us. Many foolish, ignorant Catholics never think of this; they take no care to defend themselves and thus allow the devil to inflict on them infinite harm and cause them untold sufferings. Our best, our easiest remedy is the Name of Jesus. It drives the devil flying from our sides and saves us from countless evils. Oh, Dear Readers, say constantly this all-powerful Name and the devil can do you no harm. Say it in all dangers, in all temptations. Wake up if you have been asleep. Open your eyes to the terrible enemy who is ever seeking your ruin. (O'Sullivan P., The Wonders of the Holy Name)

I can't fully stress the importance of prayer in one paragraph, but I will explain it further in Chapter Seven.

Just as there exists a holy trinity of God, Christ, and the Holy Spirit, we, humans, exist in our own trinity. It is essential that our mind, body, and spirit be in balance in order to safely explore the metaphysical realms.

NEXT . . .

In the next chapter, I will teach you how to prepare your physical body by strengthening your energy systems.

6 - ENERGY MEDICINE

When our nine energy systems are flowing healthily and working together in harmony, it makes moving between the realms much less taxing on our physical bodies. My favorite teacher of energy medicine is Donna Eden, a world-renowned healer and expert in the field. Donna teaches a daily routine that allows you to align your energy systems in less than ten minutes. If I explained all of these exercises, I would essentially be rewriting Donna's book, *Energy Medicine*. Instead, I urge you to watch Donna on YouTube. Her videos are the perfect introduction for a beginner in energy medicine.

The sheer number of videos on energy medicine can be daunting, so to keep things simple, look up the ones that cover the "Daily Energy Routine." The routine includes five important exercises: Three Thumps, Cross Crawl, Wayne Cook Posture, Crown Pull, and Zipping Up (Eden D., and D. Feinstein, _Energy Medicine_, 86).

When you keep your energy systems healthy through practicing the Daily Energy Routine, you will begin to notice your own subtle energies. Subtle energies are our body's physical response to emotions around us in our external environment. The physical manifestation of subtle energies, like anger, joy, fear, etc., varies greatly from person to person. The way I experience another's anger is a hot flash to the left side of my face that lasts a fraction of a second. For someone else, it could be a tug on their ear or a pain in their elbow. Each energy and its associated physical expression will become clear through consistent practice of energy medicine and constant attention to the nuances in our own energy fields. Every so often, there may come a day when you are unable to align your energy fields. On these days, do not allow your spirit to do any traveling. Always err on the side of caution, and wait until your fields are back in harmony.

The more you travel beyond our realm and come into contact with different spirits, the understanding of your subtle energies becomes very important. Our energies never lie to us, and attention to them will always alert you when evil is present. There have been several occasions when, with my third eye, I have seen what appeared to be a beautiful angel offering me guidance. However, when I tuned in to my subtle energies, the vibrations I felt were those of evil. Evil cannot hide because it always comes from a place of anger.

I had the fortunate opportunity to train under one of the most renowned psychics in the United States, Carol Ann Liaros. She tested my abilities and found them to be 90% accurate for reading into the future as far as six months out. I credit my accuracy to my daily practice of Donna Eden's energy medicine. When my energy systems are flowing freely and in harmony with one another, I am more in tune with my subtle energies. As instructed by Carol Ann Liaros, for a year, I logged the subtle energies I experienced along with which emotions triggered them. This vastly improved my psychic abilities.

Energy systems and meridians were first introduced in ancient Chinese medicine. Each of our energy systems runs along a meridian or energy pathway. Each of these meridians runs through an organ. If the energy is not flowing properly through a particular meridian, it is a sign that there is an energetic blockage that needs to be cleared. Failure to do so will lead to illness in the organ and person. Since the beginning of ancient Chinese medicine, Asian doctors have not been paid to treat illnesses, but to prevent them. Their profession is based on keeping the energy systems aligned so that patients stay well.

In all areas of my life, I strive to stay in a constant state of prayer. This is especially pertinent when I practice energy medicine. Throughout my routine, I recite the Hail Mary and invite Godly love to flow freely through me. When I do the Zip Up exercise, I recite part of the 23rd Psalm, "Thy rod and thy staff they comfort me." In this exercise, we run our hand up the center of our body to strengthen our central meridian and straight up the back, over our head, and down to our upper lip to strengthen our governing meridian. The front looks like a rod; the back looks like a shepherd's staff. The Zip Up exercise fits perfectly with the 23rd Psalm. When I do the Three Thumps exercise, I think of the Holy Trinity revitalizing my body as I tap on these meridians. Doing energy work and prayer on their own is wonderful, but doing them together is exceptionally powerful.

NEXT . . .

The success of the first three practices I've covered all depends on your dedication and practice. Choosing your ideal, getting control over your ego, and learning to sense subtle energies will bring you remarkably closer to God and enable you to enter a deeply profound state of prayer—the fourth and final practice.

7 - POWER OF
THE LORD'S PRAYER

In order to understand the tremendous influence that the Lord's Prayer has on your energy system, it is important to have a firm grasp on the first three concepts, which is why I saved prayer for the last section of the book. The Lord's Prayer is unequivocally the most powerful prayer in the Bible. When Jesus' disciples asked him how to pray, he gave them the Lord's Prayer. When spoken, the Lord's Prayer opens our chakras quickly, in a specific order, and to their highest level.

The Hindu religion defines the seven major energy systems as chakras. The chakras are seven distinct, spinning energy centers located in a straight line along the center of the body. Hinduism teaches that the energies flow through the chakras in a straight line, starting at the base of the spine up to the top of the head. However, ancient Egyptians, as well as Edgar Cayce, teach that the energy flows in the shape of a shepherd's hook, starting at the base of the spine and up over the head, ending at the third eye.

For our purposes, it is not necessary to understand the exact order in which the chakras flow, but rather how to safely and effectively raise our energies through the chakra system. The main objective of prayer or meditation is to raise the kundalini, or life force, through the body's chakras before releasing it into the metaphysical world. Hindu and transcendental meditators use their own will to raise their kundalini through the chakras, starting at the root chakra and flowing up to the crown. After passing through the crown, their energy expands, unprotected, into the spiritual realm. It is very dangerous to use your own will to raise up the kundalini, and there are several books warning against such practices. Those who say the Lord's Prayer when raising the kundalini are vastly more protected in the other realms.

Saying the Lord's Prayer raises the kundalini using God's will instead of human will. Reciting the Lord's Prayer allows us the safest and most protected way of meeting God. As you recite the prayer, the chakras open from your third eye, down to the base of your spine. God sends His grace down through your body's chakras to the root chakra, then back up through the chakras to the third eye before finally moving beyond into the spiritual realm.

It takes years of practice to raise up the kundalini using your own will. However, when we say the Lord's Prayer to raise up our kundalini, God comes down to meet us. With His grace and love, the kundalini flows easily and safely though our bodies and out into the psychic realms.

John Van Auken is a teacher of mysticism and ancient religions and cultures, as well as an expert in the Edgar Cayce readings. He strongly advocates using the Lord's Prayer to raise up the kundalini:

The serpent is loose to its own interests, rather than under the charm of the higher music. Keep a higher ideal, a higher purpose, a right heart, and the consciousness focused predominantly on the higher centers. Draw the Kundalini upward. (Cayce, E., and J. Van Auken, Toward a Deeper Meditation, 205)

I will now analyze the Lord's Prayer in parts, according to which energy centers are opened as Edgar Cayce explained it. Over the centuries, the text of the Lord's Prayer has been changed, but the basic meaning has not altered. In each portion of the prayer, I have capitalized the key word that opens the chakra, according to my understanding as well as that of the Cayce readings.

"Our Father, who art in HEAVEN" opens the third eye, which is the chakra located on the forehead between your eyes. In Ancient Egypt as well as in the Cayce readings, the third eye is known as the seventh and highest chakra. In Hinduism, it is the sixth chakra.

"Hallowed be thy NAME" opens the crown chakra. In Ancient Egypt and in the Cayce readings, the crown is the sixth chakra. In Hinduism the crown is the seventh chakra. During this first part of the prayer, God has moved down to meet us and has entered into our being.

"Thy kingdom come, Thy WILL" opens the fifth chakra, the throat. This chakra represents our free will. We must be willing to allow God's energy to pass through this chakra. The throat chakra is where we either accept or reject God's will and protection.

"Be done, on Earth as it is in Heaven, give us this day our daily BREAD" opens our root chakra, the first and lowest chakra located at the base of the spine. God moves directly from our will chakra at the throat, to our lowest, most earthly chakra where we have our physical roots. This chakra is where the true miracle takes place. The Holy Spirit, God's essence, mingles with our own being before moving upward, together.

"And forgive us our TRESPASSES" opens the solar plexus which is the third chakra. It holds all of our childhood memories. Few of us escape childhood without some emotional scars. We can all recall an experience that caused us to feel unsafe or lose trust in someone, thus changing how we saw the world. Commonly, our negative vibrations come from here, a hurt place in our childhood. When our energy is mixed with God's, it moves up, renewed and with a willingness to forgive.

"As we forgive those who trespass against us, and lead us not into TEMPTATION" opens the second chakra, just below the navel. You may be wondering why God would lead us backwards, from the third chakra at the solar plexus back down to the second below the navel. I believe God, knowing the shame we feel when faced with our trespasses, moves a step back to allow us to re-center ourselves. We begin to find our center as we say, "and lead us not into temptation." With the next part of the prayer, our energy shoots straight up to the fourth chakra.

"But deliver us from EVIL" opens the fourth, or heart, chakra. This opening, or transformation of the heart, is written about in Ezekiel 11:19, "and I will give them one heart, and a new spirit I will put within them. I will remove the heart of stone from their flesh and give them a heart of flesh" (STV Bible).

"For Thine is the KINGDOM" brings us again to the fifth chakra at the throat. At this point, Jesus calls us to repent one last time before entering into the psychic realm, which is one of the heavens. As given in Matthew 4:17, "The people who live in the darkness have seen a great light, and for those living in the shadowland of death, light has dawned. From then on Jesus began to preach, 'Repent, because the kingdom of Heaven has come near!'" (HSCB Bible). A truly repentant heart will only attract God's loving energy.

"And the POWER" brings us back up to the sixth chakra at the crown. At this point, God is fully within us, giving us the highest protection with which to move forward. Acts 1:8 reads, "But you will receive power when the Holy Spirit has come upon you, and you will be my witnesses in Jerusalem and in all Judea and Samaria, and to the end of the earth" (ESV).

"And the GLORY forever" finally lands back on the highest chakra—the third eye. Psalms 24:7 tells us, "Lift up your heads, O gates! And be lifted up, O ancient doors, that the King of glory may come in!" (ESV). At this point, all of your energy systems have been opened, allowing God to direct the travel of your spirit.

The Lord's Prayer should always be said during every meditation, energy healing, and spirit releasement. As long as you have chosen your ideal, trained your ego to be in alignment with God's will, and balanced your energy systems, then the power that the Lord's Prayer can offer you is immeasurable.

NEXT . . .

While the Lord's Prayer offers the strongest protection available, there are several other extremely useful prayers.

8 - POWERFUL
PROTECTION PRAYERS

In addition to the Lord's Prayer are several other important prayers that offer powerful protection in healings and spirit releasements. I will present the three that I find most helpful—St. Michael's Prayer, the Fatima Prayer, and the Hail Mary. While each of these is uniquely useful in different situations, they should always be said along with the Lord's Prayer because it offers the highest protection.

St. Michael's Prayer is a great prayer of protection. Two areas in which I frequently call on St. Michael for protection are during psychic readings and spiritual clearings. The name "Michael" means "Who is like God." St. Michael is one of the only archangels mentioned in the Bible. St. Michael's Prayer talks of the original battle in heaven as well as the one to come at the end of time. It goes as follows:

St. Michael, the Archangel,
defend us in battle.
Be our protection against the wickedness and snares of the devil.
May God rebuke him, we humbly pray;
and do you, O Prince of the heavenly host,
by the power of God cast into hell Satan and all the evil spirits
who wander through the world seeking the ruin of souls.
Amen.

The most powerful prayer in spirit releasement is the Fatima Prayer. My spiritual psychic partner, Christine, and I often refer to this prayer as the Mercy Prayer. When used during clearings, the spirits sense God's great mercy and move easily toward His light. In 1917 in rural Portugal, the Blessed Mother appeared to three shepherd children. She told them secrets of the various realms and gave them this prayer to share with the world:

O my Jesus,
forgive us our sins,
save us from the fires of hell,
and lead all souls to heaven,
especially those in most need of Thy Mercy.

Whenever I'm asked to pray for a healing, I always feel called to say the Hail Mary. After witnessing countless miracles from saying this prayer, I now believe, without a doubt, that the Hail Mary is one of the most powerful healing prayers. As children, we ran to our parents when we needed help. Through this prayer, we run to our Heavenly mother. The words of this prayer are the words spoken by the Archangel St. Gabriel when he addressed Mary on the day of Annunciation.

Hail Mary, full of Grace,
The Lord is with thee.
Blessed art Thou amongst women,
and blessed is the fruit of Thy womb,
Jesus.
Holy, Mary, Mother of God,
pray for us sinners,

now and at the hour of our death.
Amen.

Prayer is always the most powerful tool when facing evil. However, before you think of confronting evil, you must put yourself in the proper state of mind and spirit through the steps I presented in Chapter 5. When you have chosen your ideal, trained your ego to be of God's will, and strengthened and balanced your energy systems, you are then prepared to travel into realms where you might encounter evil. By using prayer in addition to all of this in your travels, you add a level of protection that only God can provide.

As a devout Catholic, church is like a second home to me, and I take full advantage of the sacraments offered by the church. It is imperative to find the faith in which you feel most comfortable and belonging. It must be one that guides you to walk in God's light. Don't look for perfection, you will not find it. Like all things led by man, no church or religion can ever be perfect. Do find God in your church and cling to Him, whatever your religion. Remember Matthew 19:26, "But Jesus beheld them, and said unto them, 'With men this is impossible; but with God all things are possible.'"

I have so much love and appreciation for my strong connection to the spiritual realms. I have mastered a level of mind-body-spirit balance that allows me to effortlessly and safely cross between the realms. I can do this because I am constantly praying. I feel unimaginably blessed to know the love and grace that pours from the other side. My goal in writing this book is for others to also find this same peace.

NEXT . . .

While in my early twenties, I experienced extremely negative psychic energies attacking me. Working through those difficult times, I learned the pricelesness of spirituality and prayer.

9 - A HOUSE BUILT ON SAND TO A HOUSE BUILT ON STONE

At the age of fifteen, I had my first download. A download is a psychic message that is delivered suddenly, giving you specific knowledge about a person or situation. I cannot remember the content of my first download because at the time I was too busy panicking. Before my first download, I thought my father and older sister were crazy when they would talk about dreaming something, then having it happen in real life. Now all I could think was, "Oh my God, I'm crazy like they are!"

By the time I turned eighteen, I was much less freaked out by my psychic abilities and had even begun experimenting with them. I started remote viewing, reading tarot cards, reading tea leaves, sensing bodies for illness, and sending up protection, just to name a few. For the following three years, like a sponge, I soaked up all the information I could about the occult. It interested me far more than my college education ever did. I even considered dabbling in magic, but my gut told me to keep away from it.

I felt like a psychic junkie—the more I learned, the more I desired to learn. I felt superior, like my ego was riding first class while everyone else's rode coach. Then out of nowhere, I got sick. There seemed to be nothing physically wrong with me, but I was gripped by such unimaginable pain that I believed I must have been dying. For three months, the pain steadily increased by the day. At times, I could barely walk across a room without becoming exhausted and feeling like I was on the brink of a heart attack.

Christmas came and I was feeling as miserable as usual, until a little after ten in the morning. It was like someone flicked a switch and I was suddenly myself, a vibrant twenty-year-old once again! Minutes into my celebration, my family received a phone call letting us know my grandfather had died a few minutes before. I was shocked by the realization that it had been my grandfather's pain I had been picking up on for the previous three months.

Over the years, I had three more episodes of chest pain preceding someone's death. Luckily, they were never as intense as the first time. I felt frustrated, knowing someone, but not who, was going to die and I was unable to help. Then it got worse . . .

As soon as I entered the same room as someone who wasn't feeling well, I was hit with their physical ailments. The only reprieve from my now constant pain was a game I invented. As if solving a mystery, I would tune into find whom the pain was coming from, so I could offer them an aspirin for the both of us. Often people were confused how I knew of their pain, but rarely did they refuse the aspirin.

Physical ailments were not enough to deter me from exploring the psychic realm. I continued to read and learn everything I could to better understand this vast and unexplored territory. One of the last things I learned was how to move my spirit in and out of my physical body. I could do this travel without anyone around me noticing. The only thing that might have given me away was how quiet I would become. Those who know me well know that being quiet is no easy feat for me.

Part of this newfound skill was the ability to see energy. With my third eye, I could see the energy surrounding and flowing between people. These energies were all different strengths, colors, and emotions.

One day at a family gathering, I saw someone sending hateful, negative energy at my mother. To protect her, I sent my spirit to block this energy. I felt sick and sluggish for days. Today, I know that I should have called on God to protect my mother, but at the time, I had no spirituality behind my basic religious beliefs. Shortly after this experience with my mother is when I reached my breaking point.

I was beyond tired—tired of feeling sick, tired of feeling others' pain, tired of knowing people were going to die and being unable to help. But deeper than that, I was angry, angry at God for giving me these gifts but not giving me a way to help. I finally told God that I no longer wanted this gift and to take it away. No sooner did the words leave my lips than I regretted them. I begged God to give my gift back, and, though he heard, he made me wait. For the next twenty-five years, God held my gifts while I developed my mental, physical, and spiritual self.

In my youth, my abilities were built upon a foundation of sand that quickly fell apart. The second time around, God was my center, my foundation, and my rock.

Through God, my abilities have tenfold the power that they did in my youth. More importantly, I'm safe in God's arms as I travel beyond this body. And it is for this reason that I was motivated to write this book—I want you, dear reader, to journey safely in that other realm with God at your side.

References

Alban, F., *Fatima Priest*. Pound Ridge, NY: Good Counsel Publications, 1997.

American Standard Bible. New York: Thomas Nelson and Sons, 1901.

Baldwin, W., *Spirit Releasement Therapy: A Technique Manual*. Terra Alta, WV: Headline Books, 1992.

Cayce, E., *God's Other Door and the Continuity of Life*. Whitefish, MT: Kessinger Publishing, 2010.

Cayce, E., and J. Van Auken, *Toward a Deeper Meditation*. Virginia Beach, VA: A.R.E. Press, 1992.

Eden, D., and D. Feinstein, Energy Medicine. New York: Tarcher/Putnam, 1998.

Liaros, C. A., *Intuition Made Easy*. Scottsdale, AZ: Cloudbank Creations, 2003.

Mary of Agreda, *The Mystical City of God The Divine History and Life of the Virgin Mother of God, Manifested to Mary of Agreda for the Encouragement of Men*. London: Catholic Way, 2013.

Michaelsen, J., *The Beautiful Side of Evil*. Eugene, OR: Harvest House, 1982.

O'Sullivan, P., *The Wonders of the Holy Name*. Lisbon: Edições do Corpo, 1946.

Parente, A., *Send Me Your Guardian Angel: Padre Pio*. Our Lady, 1984.

Pratnicka, W., *Possessed by Ghosts: Exorcisms in the 21st Century*. Ashland, OH: Atlasbooks Dist Serve, 2006.

Puryear, H. B., and M. A. Thurston, *Meditation and the Mind of Man*. Virginia Beach, VA: A.R.E. Press, 1975.

Reed, H. "Battered Boundaries, Transpersonal Counseling for Intrusive Psychic Experiences." Accessed October 20, 2015. http://www.creativespirit.net/noboundaries/batteredb oundaries.htm.

Reed, H., and B. English, *The Intuitive Heart: How To Trust Your Intuition for Guidance and Healing*. Virginia Beach, VA: A.R.E. Press, 2000.

Sechrist, E., *Meditation: Gateway to Light*. Virginia Beach, VA: A.R.E. Press, 1972.

Sharamon, S., and B. Baginski, *The Chakra Handbook: From Basic Understanding to Practical Applications*. Aitrang, Germany: Windpferd Verlagsgesellschaft, 1988.

Sugrue, T., *The Story of Edward Cayce: There Is a River*. Virginia Beach, VA: A.R.E. Press, 1942.

Targ, R., *Limitless Mind: A Guide to Remote Viewing and Transformation of Consciousness*. Novato, CA: New World Library, 2010.

Van Aukens, J., *Edgar Cayce and the Kabbalah: Resources for Soulful Living*. Virginia Beach, VA: A.R.E. Press, 2010.

About the Author

Nora Truscello is a certified Intuitive Heart Instructor and a proven expert in delivering accurate information, leaving participants of lectures, as well as private clients, extremely satisfied with her spiritual counsel. Nora has been tested and scored over 90% accuracey in psychic readings up to six months into the future. Nora lives with her husband and enjoys her three sons, their wives, and grandchildren visiting regularly.

13757489R00053

Printed in Great Britain
by Amazon.co.uk, Ltd.,
Marston Gate.